SEVEN SEAS ENTERTAINMENT PRESENTS

Happy Kanako's Killer

story and art by TOSHIYA WAKABAYASHI

TRANSLATION
Wesley O'Donnell

LETTERING
Carolina Hernández Mendoza

COVER AND LOGO DESIGN
Hanase Qi

PROOFREADER
Kurestin Armada

COPY EDITOR
Dawn Davis

EDITOR
J.P. Sullivan

PREPRESS TECHNICIAN
Rhiannon Rasmussen-Silverstein

PRODUCTION ASSOCIATE
Christa Miesner

PRODUCTION MANAGER
Lissa Pattillo

MANAGING EDITOR
Julie Davis

ASSOCIATE PUBLISHER
Adam Arnold

PUBLISHER
Jason DeAngelis

ISBN: 978-1-64827-798-6
Printed in Canada
First Printing: August 2021

10 9 8 7 6 5 4 3 2 1

////// READING DIRECTIONS //////

This book reads from *right to left*, Japanese style. If this is your first time reading manga, you start reading from the top right panel on each page and take it from there. If you get lost, just follow the numbered diagram here. It may seem backwards at first, but you'll get the hang of it! Have fun!!

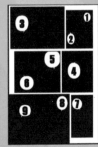

I'll come charging back with more happy tales so hang in there ☆

From
Toshiya Wakabayashi

Thank you for reading!! I hope you enjoyed it even a little bit!!

Special thanks to
Joachim Larsen

Happy Kanako's
Killer Life

☆──────────────── **To Be Continued!**

BUT IT SEEMS YOU'RE BUSY TODAY...

ABOUT YOUR FORMER BOSS.

I WAS HOPING WE COULD HAVE A CHAT...

COULD WE HAVE YOUR PHONE NUMBER?

IF WE HAD THIS DISCUSSION LATER.

MAYBE IT WOULD WORK BETTER...

WELL...

UH...

THANK YOU VERY MUCH!!

TH...

Intimidating. ────────────────────── ★

Intimidating.

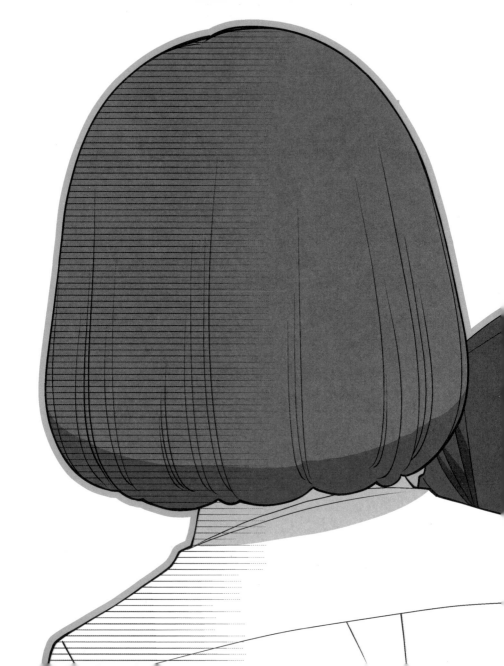

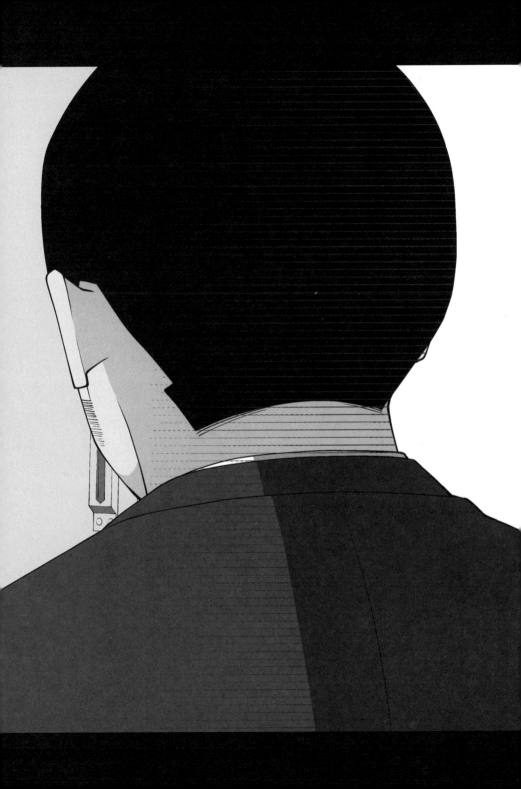

THIS IS THE PLACE.

HUH?

DON'T I COME OFF FRIENDLY?

REMEMBER, SHE RESIGNED DUE TO HARASSMENT.

WATCH WHAT YOU SAY TO HER.

NO, NO, NO.

I'M LIKE THE NICE OLDER-BROTHER TYPE!!

NO, YOU'RE INTIMIDATING.

YOU'RE BIG, LOUD, AND BRASH.

KER-CHAK

I'LL JUST SMILE AND IT'LL ALL BE--

HMM...

WHEN GOING OUT WITH A FRIEND?

WHAT SHOULD I WEAR...

WOULD THAT BE WEIRD?

I DON'T WANT TO DRESS TOO FANCY AND GIVE OFF THE WRONG IMPRESSION.

I DON'T EVEN HAVE ANY!!

WAIT.

FANCY CLOTHES?

☆——— Fast Fashion to the rescue!

This ——————————————————— moron. ☆

THERE'S THIS OLD URBAN LEGEND.

ABOUT A GROUP OF ASSASSINS.

IT'S SAID THEY ORIGINALLY WORKED FOR THE YAKUZA...

BUT THEN THEY STARTED ACCEPTING OTHER JOBS.

I SEE...

AND THE WEAPON USED IN THE TRAIN INCIDENT WAS A GUN.

NOT SOMETHING A RANDOM SLASHER CAN EASILY GET THEIR HANDS ON...

AREN'T I AMAZING?

AREN'T I??

☆ ———————— **This guy really gets on my nerves.**

But there's no way it would be the new hire, right? ──── ☆

COME ON. DISAPPEARANCES, UNEXPLAINED DEATHS...

DO YOU KNOW HOW MANY OF THOSE WE GET?

TRUE...

AND YET HIS HEAD INJURIES WERE WAY MORE SEVERE THAN NORMAL.

THE GUY DIED BY FALLING OFF THE ROOF.

BUT FOR THIS SUICIDE...

BUT HOW MANY PEOPLE COMMITTING SUICIDE DIVE HEAD-FIRST?

THAT WOULD HAVE DONE IT.

SURE, HE COULD HAVE TAKEN A NOSEDIVE.

BEFORE THE FALL.

I THINK HE WAS KILLED.

☆————— But there's no way it was a sniper, right?

TAKEHARA-KUN...

JUST SPIT IT OUT.

YOU'RE PISSING ME OFF.

A LOT OF OTHER GUYS WITH *ISSUES* HAVE VANISHED.

AND THIS SUICIDE WAS EXACTLY ONE MONTH PRIOR.

THE GUY KILLED ON THE TRAIN WAS A HABITUAL GROPER.

THERE HAVE BEEN OTHER INCIDENTS IN THE PAST MONTH.

SO, YOU'RE SAYING...

THIS SUICIDE...

MAY HAVE BEEN THE MURDERER'S FIRST KILL?

HEH HEH.

He's so annoying. ─────────── ☆

FROM WHAT I HEARD...

A FEW DAYS BEFORE HE DIED...

HE LIKED TO PUSH HIS WEIGHT AROUND THE OFFICE.

HE FORCED AN EMPLOYEE TO RESIGN.

SO, WHAT I'M SAYING IS...

SMELLS A BIT FISHY, DON'T YOU THINK?

THIS WHOLE SUICIDE THING.

SO YOU THINK...

THIS HAS SOMETHING TO DO WITH THE PERSON WHO RESIGNED?

Heh.

★———————————————————————— Ugh!

Bonus

LAST MONTH...

A GUY JUMPED TO HIS DEATH.

REMEMBER THAT?

BUT IT WAS WRITTEN OFF AS A SUICIDE FROM OVERWORK.

THERE WAS NO NOTE...

WAS A MALE IN HIS FORTIES WORKING FOR AN AD AGENCY.

THE DECEASED...

YOU THINK IT'S RELATED TO THE TRAIN MURDER?

WHAT ABOUT IT, TAKEHARA-KUN?

AND?

A dangerous detective! ────────────── ☆

Happy Kanako's
Killer Life

Happy Kanako's
Killer Life

Burning,
raging
in-fur-
no!!

☆ —————————————————— **I'm so glad I took this job!**

YOU'VE CERTAINLY LIGHTENED UP, SAKURAI.

I WONDER IF THAT'S ALSO DUE TO HER?

BOSS...

SHE STILL HAS SOME USE TO US.

THE STUPID RUBS OFF ON THEM.

AND WHEN PEOPLE LOOK AT YOU...

YOU MAY BE A NATURAL, BUT YOU'RE ALSO AN IDIOT.

NISHINO.

WHAT AM I GOING TO DO WITH THIS IDIOT?

SO, I GUESS I HAVE TO DECIDE.

I'M REALLY GLAD...

THAT I FINALLY FOUND A PLACE WHERE I FELT LIKE I BELONGED.

SO, THIS IS IT?

IT WAS SHORT, BUT NICE WHILE IT LASTED.

YOU DID IT AGAIN.

. . . . . .

I JUST... I HAVE NO EXCUSE...

I...I'M SORRY...

OH, FOR HELL'S SNAKE!!

THIS TIME, HE'S REALLY PISSED...!!

KER-CHAK

IT'S FINE.

I'M THE ONE WHO HIRED YOU.

IT'S MY FAULT.

I'M GETTING FIRED.

AH...

☆ ——— Thanks for reading *Happy Kanako's Killer Life.*

Morals? What're those? ─────────────────── ☆

THAT'LL MAKE IT HARDER TO GET WORK DONE.

IT'LL JUST CAUSE MORE TROUBLE FOR EVERYONE.

OH, RIGHT...

IF WE GET TOO WELL-KNOWN, THE COPS WILL GET INVOLVED.

I SHOULD JUST GO BACK TO BEING WHO I WAS...

BEING NOBODY.

Uh, go for it!!

Hey, do you mind if we film you?

I GUESS I ALWAYS WAS...

JUST ANOTHER BORING NOBODY.

AND WE'RE GOING TO TELL HER EVERYTHING SHE'S DOING WRONG!!

WE'RE BACK WITH ANOTHER WANNABE MUSICIAN...

WELCOME BACK TO CHANNEL SUNGLASSES!!

TWITCH

☆ ──────────── Someone's always shooting here.

THE MYSTERY OF "K" ENDURES.

NO ONE KNOWS WHO HE REALLY IS!

THANKS TO HIM...

WE'VE CERTAINLY GOT MORE JOBS LATELY.

WOW!! REALLY?!

THAT'S PRETTY AWESOME!!

NOBODY KNOWS WHO HE COULD BE...

BUT EVEN OTHER FIRMS ARE GETTING MORE WORK.

YOU IDIOT.

IF WE STAND OUT TOO MUCH...

THE BOSS WILL BE FURIOUS.

He's Feline Fur~ious~ ——————————— ☆

☆ —————————————— **She also sent her a lame sticker.**

It's me, big-sis Kanako! ────────────────── ☆

I CAN'T DO ANYTHING OUTSIDE OF KILLING PEOPLE...

WAAAH! WAAAH!

BUT I'M STILL JUST CAUSING TROUBLE AROUND THE OFFICE.

I MAY BE GAINING A REPUTATION IN THE UNDERWORLD...

WHAT IF WE GO OUT AGAIN...

AND THEN SHE NEVER CONTACTS ME AFTERWARDS?

WAAAH!

WAAAH!

AND SCREWING THINGS UP WITH FRIENDS IS EVEN SCARIER THAN GETTING KILLED AT WORK.

SHUT THAT KID UP!!

WHAT'S WITH THE RACKET?!

HEY!!

IF ONLY I COULD SETTLE THIS WITH MY GUN.

UGH...

☆ —————— Shut that big baby up with one shot!

THANKS TO THAT UNDERWORLD RUMOR...

I'VE GAINED A BIT OF CONFIDENCE.

Yoshioka Kiyomi

Are you free this Sunday? Maybe we could go out somewhere?

IT'LL MAKE HER THINK I'M MORE WITH IT?

MAYBE IF I RESPOND WITH A STICKER...

BUT IN EVERYDAY SITUATIONS...

I'M STILL HOPELESS.

Are you we could go out som

OK

TRMBLE

TRMBLE

I JUST DON'T KNOW IF IT'S APPROPRIATE OR NOT!!

I'll just say it works for me...or something.

I CAN'T DO IT!!

That's also why she's not using emojis. ──────☆

☆ ──────── **Make sure you don't blab to my parents~**

Time to die~ ─────────────────────────────────── ☆

He doesn't look too busy.

IN THE UNDER-WORLD...

THERE'S RUMOR OF AN ASSASSIN KNOWN AS "K."

NEWBIE.

WE'VE GOT A JOB.

AH... IS IT...

WITH THE YAKUZA?

YEAH.

YOU BETTER GET USED TO WORKING WITH THEM.

THAT MEANS...

IF "K" SHOWS UP...

EVERYONE WOULD THINK IT WAS TOTALLY AWESOME.

THIS IS UN-BUN-LIEVABLE!!

I'M NOT SOME STAR!!

But maybe I should touch up my makeup. ───────── ☆

MAYBE WE SHOULD GET DOWN TO BUSINESS.

YOU SEEM PRETTY TIGHT-LIPPED.

HMM...

I THOUGHT...

I WAS ALWAYS GOING TO BE PLAIN SIMPLE ME.

WAIT... WHAT'S THE ARMA-DEALIO?!

I SHOULDN'T BE HAPPY ABOUT THIS.

BUT NOW...

I'VE SOMEHOW BECOME FAMOUS.

I'M TOTALLY STOKED!!

I'm amazing!!

WOOOO-HOOOO!!

THMP

THMP

THMP

⭐ ———————— **And not just at dancing!**

THEY SAY HE CAN DO ANY JOB.

THAT HE'S SOME SUPER-SKILLED ASSASSIN.

I SAW THAT TRAIN HIT ON THE NEWS.

RUMOR AROUND THE UNDERWORLD IS SOME GUY KNOWN AS K DID IT.

PEOPLE ARE THINKING IT PROBABLY STANDS FOR KILLER.

NO ONE KNOWS HIS ACTUAL NAME OR AGE.

OR EVEN WHERE THE NAME "K" COMES FROM.

DOES THIS K WORK FOR YOU GUYS?

SO LAY IT ON ME.

I DON'T KNOW ANYTHING ABOUT IT!!

WHAT?

THAT ALL SOUNDS CRAZY!

I don't really follow celebrities. ────────────── ☆

HUH?

ARE YOU WITH...?

NO... IT'S FINE, JUST...

YOU LOOK JUST LIKE ANY OTHER OFFICE GIRL.

AH... YES.

SORRY ABOUT THIS...

I'VE GOTTA HURRY UP AND GET USED TO IT.

I'M GONNA CROAK!!

BUT THIS IS ALSO PART OF THE JOB.

EMPLOY AN ASSASSIN KNOWN AS "K"?

SO.

DOES YOUR FIRM...

I'M GETTING THE HANG OF BEING A HITMAN...

BUT I STILL SUCK AT TALKING TO PEOPLE.

WHAT?!

YOU WANT ME TO MEET WITH THE YAKUZA, ALONE??

WHAT IF HE GETS ANGRY OR SOMETHING...?

BUT...

AND SAKURAI IS BUSY CHASING HIM DOWN.

THE MEDIATOR DISAPPEARED.

YOU CAN KILL HIM.

IF ANYTHING HAPPENS...

WELL, OKAY.

EHHHHH.

I kind of hope something happens now! ─────── ☆

Happy Kanako's Killer Life

No way, no way! What a croc'!!

Happy Kanako's
Killer Life

Here
we go,
here
we go,
here
we
foxin'
go!!

AND YET SOMEHOW, I INSPIRED SOMEONE.

THAT WAS SURPRISING.

I THOUGHT PEOPLE JUST CONSIDERED ME A KLUTZ.

I SHOULD LEARN TO LIKE MYSELF MORE.

I WAS THINKING I WANTED TO CHANGE MYSELF...

BUT MAYBE INSTEAD...

I DON'T GET IT!!

☆ ——————————————— **And that's okay.**

Effort, my one saving grace~ ──────────────────── ☆

PROBABLY WISHING SHE DIDN'T INVITE ME OUT.

Phew!! That was good!!

I'M THE WORST.

SHE HAS TO THINK I'M A MESS.

WE'LL NEVER SEE EACH OTHER AGAIN.

CHANCES ARE GOOD...

BUT THAT'S FINE.

SAY.

DO YOU WANT TO GO OUT AGAIN SOMETIME?

!!

She's way too nice!

R-RIGHT...

EVERYONE'S THOUGHT THAT AT LEAST ONCE!!

AH... SORRY...

THAT WAS JUST A JOKE. A JOKE!

I MEAN, MAYBE ONCE OR TWICE!!

REALLY?!

LIAR.

SHE TOTALLY HASN'T.

I'M GOING TO TRY THE SAKE!!

WHAT ABOUT ANOTHER DRINK?!!

C'MON STOP BRINGING DOWN THE MOOD.

GOTTA PUT BACK ON THE HAPPY FACE!!

Drink, drink, drink it all away! ━━━━━━━━━━━ ☆

What? That was forever ago!

IT'S BECAUSE I HATED COMPARING MYSELF TO HER.

Well, you were the class president.

NOW I'M REMEMBERING...

WHY I LOST CONTACT WITH KIYOMI-CHAN.

I'M ALWAYS JUST SCREWING THINGS UP.

YOU'RE AMAZING.

SHE'D NEVER HATE HERSELF LIKE THAT.

IF IT WERE KIYOMI-CHAN...

JUST PUT ME OUT OF MY...

CRAP, THE CAT'S OUT OF THE BAG.

★ ———————————————— **Instant mood killer~**

Depression Switch ON. ────────────────── ★

☆ ——————————————————————— **Opening old wounds!**

Totes. ─────────────────────────── ☆

C'MON, WE WERE CLASSMATES, WEREN'T WE?

CALL ME KIYOMI.

UH...

YOSHIOKA-SAN?

I HOPE SHE DOESN'T WANT TO CATCH UP...

THINGS GOT AWKWARD AFTER WE GRADUATED MIDDLE SCHOOL.

TOTAL OPPOSITES. WE WERE JUST FRIENDLY BECAUSE WE SAT NEXT TO EACH OTHER.

YEAH, BUT YOU WERE CLASS PRESIDENT AND AN HONORS STUDENT!

MAYBE IF YOU'RE FREE, WE COULD GET DINNER TOGETHER??

SO?

ARE YOU ON YOUR WAY HOME?

SURE!!

EH...

UH...

☆ ———————————————— **She doesn't know how to say no.**

Bonus

IT'S AFTER FIVE ON A FRIDAY.

BEFORE ANYONE ASKS IF I WANNA GO DRINKING...

I'M GETTING OUT OF HERE TO GO HOME.

NEWBIE...

AH!

NICE WORK THIS WEEK!!

......

YOU, TOO.

HA!! I'M FREE!!

OH?

IS THAT YOU, KANAKO-CHAN?

I'VE GOT THE WHOLE NIGHT TO MYSELF! I'M GONNA...

Who are you? ──────────────────── ☆

Happy Kanako's
Killer Life

"I'M DOING MY BEST."

"I DID A GOOD JOB."

IT'S TIME FOR A CHANGE.

I NEED TO START PRAISING MYSELF MORE.

MAYBE A NICE OUTFIT, OR...

I'VE GOT THE MONEY.

MAYBE I'LL GET MYSELF A PRESENT!!

RIGHT...!!

Mighty Morphing Killer Rangers!!

I'M TRANSFORM-ING!!

WOOOO-HOOOOO!!

★ —— Become who you want to be.

I'd be lion to say I'm not jealous. ────────────☆

AND THEN... I STARTED BELIEVING THEM.

I'M A DINOSAURUS MESS.

PEOPLE HAVE ALWAYS TOLD ME I WAS SLOW.

TO GET MORE SELF-CONFIDENCE?

WHAT CAN I DO...

SHP

BRAZENLY STEAL THINGS LIKE THAT?

WHOA, HOW CAN SHE JUST...

 ——————————— I'm too scared to do bad things.

WELL, NEWBIE.

LOOKS LIKE YOU CAN HANDLE JOBS ON YOUR OWN FROM NOW ON.

I'VE SPENT A WHOLE MONTH AS A HITMAN.

I'M MOSTLY SETTLED IN, BUT...

WHAT ARE YOU BABBLING?

STOP WORRYING.

EH? OH...NO, NO...

I'M STILL LEARNING...

HAVE SOME CONFIDENCE.

WE'LL ALL WORRY.

OTHERWISE...

THAT TROUBLED BECAUSE OF ME?!!

ARE THEY ALL REALLY...

Absolutely zero self-confidence! ──────── ☆

☆ ——————The roof, the roof, the roof is on fire!

WHY IS THIS OVER EASY EGG STILL RUNNY?

HEY, WHAT THE HECK IS THIS?

OKAY... I'LL CALL SAKURAI-SAN!!

JUST TO MAKE SURE THE PLAN IS SOUND!!

WHAT ARE YOU TRYING TO SERVE ME?!

HOW CAN YOU EVEN CALL THIS COOKING?!!

SURE, SAKURAI-SAN MIGHT BE ANNOYED.

BUT THAT'S BETTER THAN CAUSING MORE WORK BY SCREWING UP.

But he still said you could handle this.

So he at least approves of you.

You think Sakurai doesn't like you?

He doesn't really like anyone.

OFF...

I'm going to do it myself. ────────────────── ☆

BUT THIS TIME, IT'S ALL ON ME!!

THEY'VE HELPED TO HIDE THE EVIDENCE AND CLEAN UP THE BODIES.

UP TILL NOW I'VE ALWAYS BEEN WITH THE BOSS OR SAKURAI-SAN.

I DON'T WANT TO SCREW THIS UP!!

BUT THIS TIME, THEY'RE RELYING ON ME...

I WAS JUST A TAGALONG. THERE WASN'T ANYTHING RIDING ON ME.

ON THE OTHER JOBS...

HEY!

WATER!

THINKING ABOUT IT JUST MAKES IT WORSE!!

UGH!!

★ ——————— **She's the weak under pressure type.**

PROBABLY IT'S BECAUSE OF THE NEWS...

BUT WE'VE GOTTEN MORE WORK LATELY.

NISHINO.

CAN YOU HANDLE THIS?

NOPE...

HE'S ON ANOTHER ASSIGNMENT.

IS SAKURAI-SAN ALREADY ON SITE?

AH... SURE!!

I'M STILL A BIT UNEASY ABOUT THIS...

BUT SAKURAI SAID YOU COULD HANDLE IT.

IT'S TIME TO GIVE IT A SHOT GOING SOLO.

Y...

YES, SIR...

OMG, this is turtley nuts!! ─────────────── ☆

ALL THAT WORK WRITING A SUICIDE LETTER ABOUT BEING DISCOVERED PEEPING...

ALL GONE TO WASTE.

SOMETIMES JOBS DON'T GO AS PLANNED.

YEAH, I NOTICED.

I SCREWED UP...

I...I'M SORRY!!

JUST PART OF BEING A PRO.

AND THEN YOU HAVE TO PLAY IT BY EAR.

WHOA!!

YOU CAN SEE THE STARS SO CLEARLY OUT HERE!!

☆ ——————————————— **Being a pro has its perks!**

IS THAT A GUN?! A REAL ONE??

HUH... WHAT THE...?!

DON'T RUN.

CREAK...

BUT I SHOULD FINISH HIM OFF WITH THE DRUGS AS PLANNED.

THIS MUST BE THE PEEPER WE'RE AFTER.

I ALREADY TOOK THE ONE QUICK SHOT...

I WAS JUST TRYING TO CHECK IF THERE WAS ANYONE WEIRD IN HERE!!

YOU JUST SHOT MY PHONE?!

ARE YOU AN UNDERCOVER COP?!

NO... WAIT!!

I MEANT TO USE THE DRUGS!!

PSHEW

AHHHHH!!

Just walk it off! ───────────────── ☆

I'VE GOT TO PAY MORE ATTENTION TO THE JOB...

I'VE RODENT THINGS AGAIN...

I GOT SAKURAI-SAN IN TROUBLE.

LIKE SAKURAI-SAN...

I'VE GOT TO BE MORE COMPOSED.

I CAN'T LET MY EMOTIONS CONTROL ME.

ESPECIALLY MY SURROUNDINGS.

SLIDE...

KRAK

PSHEW

☆ —————— **Now for the rest of me to catch on!**

SO THE NEWS...

IS THINKING IT WAS A TERRORIST OR RANDOM ATTACK.

電車内で発砲 男性死亡

MY LAST HIT MADE THE NEWS.

NO ONE IS PAYING ATTENTION TO ANYONE ELSE.

WELL...YOU KNOW HOW IT IS ON TRAINS.

THAT'S PRETTY GOOD.

TAKING SOMEONE OUT ON A CROWDED TRAIN WITHOUT BEING NOTICED...

ARE YOU TAKING THIS SERIOUSLY?

BUT YOU SHOULDN'T HAVE TAKEN THAT CHANCE!

WE'RE SORRY.

．．．．．

Give him the puppy dog eyes. ────────────────── ☆

THE SUN'S ALREADY GONE DOWN!

WHAT?!!

HOW'S IT ALREADY SO LATE?!

HOW COULD I BE SO IN-E-FISH-ENT?!!

ALL I DID WAS CLEAN AND LOOK AT THE INTERNET!!

AND I WANTED TO DO SOMETHING MEANINGFUL TODAY!!

AND I'VE GOT WORK TOMORROW...

I AT LEAST WANTED TO GO OUT SOMEWHERE...

BUT NOW IT'S ALREADY DARK OUT...

SUNDAY IS MY DAY!!

BUT I'M STILL BORN TO RUN!!

☆ ————————— **Tonight I'm living for myself!**

Goodnight Spinosauruzzzzz ———————————— ☆

☆———————You talk to yourself more when you're lonely.

009

NOW THAT I WORK AS A HITMAN...

I'VE SUDDENLY GOT WEEKENDS OFF.

Let's go!! Transform!!

I HAVEN'T WATCHED A KID'S SHOW IN FOREVER.

BACK AT MY LAST JOB...

I'D NEVER BE UP THIS EARLY ON A SUNDAY.

OR MAYBE I WOULDN'T EVEN BE HOME YET...

MIGHTY MORPHING...

KILLER RANGERS!!

SUNDAY MORNING...

IS TOTALLY AWESOME.

Everybody loves cartoons ──────────────── ☆

Happy Kanako's
Killer Life

Happy Kanako's
Killer Life

I've got the koala-fications!!

☆ ——————————— **This company's full of nice people.**

WELL... A SENSE OF PURPOSE IS GOOD...

BUT THIS IS A JOB WHERE YOU HAVE TO STEEL YOUR HEART.

I...I GUESS SO...

Maybe flattery will get me out of this!!

YOU'RE SO NICE!!

TO LET SOMEONE DOWN EASILY, RIGHT, SAKURAI-SAN?

SO YOU MUST SOMETIMES HAVE TO STEEL YOUR HEART...

SHOULDN'T HAVE SAID THAT.

CRAP...

Whelp, I'm done for. ──────────────────── ☆

☆ ——— **But is this really a good way to find fulfillment?**

BUT I'LL GET USED TO IT SOON ENOUGH!!

PROBABLY...

I...I TOTALLY HAVE THE TEMPERAMENT!!

SURE I'M CRYING AND LAUGHING NOW...

NO... I MEAN...

SURE, THE MONEY'S A PART OF IT, BUT...

WHY DO YOU WANT THIS JOB SO BADLY?

THE MONEY?

I CAN REALLY FEEL LIKE *MYSELF*, Y'KNOW?

WHEN I KILL SOMEONE...

WHAT THE HECK ARE YOU SAYING?

I know, right? ──────────────────── ☆

BUT I'LL START PUTTING IN MORE EFFORT.

I MEAN, I KNOW I'VE BEEN A PAIN SO FAR...

O...OF COURSE!! I CAN DO THIS!!

YOU CAN'T KEEP THAT UP AS A PRO.

IT WAS JUST ONE KILL AND YET YOU'RE CRYING, YOU'RE LAUGHING...

YOU JUST SEEM TO BE GETTING TOO INVESTED.

MAYBE YOU JUST DON'T HAVE THE NERVE.

I KNOW A CRAPPY BOSS RAN YOU OUT OF YOUR LAST JOB.

AH... IS HE...

IS THIS HIS WAY OF TELLING ME TO QUIT...?!!

☆ ——————————— I mean, he's not wrong, but...!

Bonus

I DRANK TOO MUCH AFTER WORK.

I...I'M... SORRY...

URGH!!

ARE YOU ALL RIGHT?

BLEEEGH!!

BUT NOW I'M BEING A BURDEN EVEN OUTSIDE OF WORK...

I WAS TRYING TO HOLD IT IN UNTIL I WAS ALONE.

AW, C'MON, SPARROW ME!

ARE YOU SURE THIS IS THE LINE OF WORK FOR YOU?

HEY.

Pretty sure he's pissed. ─────────── ☆

Happy Kanako's
Killer Life

Oh, for hell's snake!!

Happy Kanako's Killer Life

☆ ————————— I'm going to kill all the bad things in the world!

HUH? WAIT.

IF YOU TAKE HIM OUT HERE, YOU'LL BE FOUND OUT.

SAKURAI-SAN...THAT BASTARD'S DOING IT AGAIN.

HE WON'T SEE ME.

SHE MIGHT FEEL EMBARRASSED FOR BEING SO WEAK.

SHE MIGHT END UP BLAMING HERSELF.

BUT I CAN'T JUST LET HIM DO IT!

THAT GIRL MIGHT THINK IT WAS HER OWN FAULT SHE GOT MOLESTED!

WHO HATE THEMSELVES EVERY DAY, LIKE I USED TO!

THERE TO BE MORE PEOPLE...

I DON'T WANT...

DO YOU THINK YOU CAN ERASE YOUR PRESENCE?

HEY.

I've got the koalafications! ———————————— ☆

ALL WE WERE TOLD WAS HIS M.O. AND WHAT TRAIN LINE...

BUT IF WE CAN CONFIRM IT'S HIM, WE CAN TAKE HIM OUT.

THAT PERV...

MIGHT BE THE GUY WE'VE GOT A HIT ON.

YES!! I'LL FOLLOW HIM AND THEN CONTACT YOU!!

HUH?! UH...

ARE YOU LISTENING?

TRACK HIM UNTIL YOU'RE SOMEWHERE QUIET, AND THEN...

ME- SPHINX HE'S GONNA DIE!

BUT NOW THAT I'M AN ASSASSIN...

I WOULD HAVE BEEN AFRAID OF THE GROPER GETTING VIOLENT, OR EMBARRASSED BY PEOPLE STARING AT ME...

BACK BEFORE I BECAME A HITMAN...

Target Locked.

008

ON A CROWDED MORNING TRAIN...

I WAS ATTACKED BY A GROPER.

HEY...

HEY! STOP THAT!!

BEFORE, WHEN I WASN'T A HITMAN...

I'D HAVE JUST PUT UP WITH IT, BUT NOW...

IF I WAS GOING TO DO ANYTHING, I'D HAVE PICKED SOMEONE CUTER!

WHAT ARE YOU TALKING ABOUT?

HUH?

Maybe you should ride in the women-only cars...

Tch... What? Is this some scam attempt?

KILL KILL KILL KILL KILL KILL KILL KILL KILL KILL KILL KILL KILL ☆

 It's nice helping people in need!

WHA?!

EH, SAKURAI-SAN?!

WHAT'RE YOU DOING HERE??

WE TAKE THE SAME TRAIN HOME.

BUT YOU'RE STILL TOO NAÏVE.

YOU CAN'T BE A PRO LIKE THAT.

NEWBIE.

YOU MAY BE A NATURAL...

AND JUST KEEP MOANING ABOUT IT...

IT'D BE BEST TO QUIT NOW.

IF YOU'RE NOT GOING TO DUMP THE SWEETNESS...

BUT INSTEAD GO FIND IT MYSELF?

IS HE TELLING ME...

THAT I SHOULDN'T WAIT FOR A JOB WHERE I HELP PEOPLE...

Talk about a stretch. ——————————————☆

KILLING SOMEONE JUST TO HELP SOMEONE ELSE?

OF COURSE NOT.

I GET IT, BUT YOU'VE GOT TO STOP THINKING THAT WAY.

WE DON'T WORK FOR FREE.

WE'RE NOT A RUNNING A CHARITY HERE.

LISTEN UP, NISHINO.

JUST 'CAUSE SOMEONE'S IN TROUBLE DOESN'T MEAN I CAN GO OFF KILLING PEOPLE...

I GUESS SO...

WE'RE NOT SUPERHEROES, AFTER ALL.

YOU DON'T SEEM CONVINCED.

☆————— **Fancy beetle-ing you here.**

SINCE BECOMING A HITMAN...

WORK'S GOTTEN A LOT MORE BEARABLE.

BUT IT'S BROUGHT SOME NEW STRUGGLES.

BUT WE STILL CAN'T TAKE IT AS A RETURN...

I DIDN'T OPEN IT! IT'S PRACTICALLY NEW!!

YEAH, I BOUGHT IT, BUT I DIDN'T EAT IT!!

LIKE. I. SAID!!

HUH?! WHAT??

AND YOU DON'T HAVE A RECEIPT, SO...

ARE YOU CALLIN' ME A LIAR?!

THAT'S NOT MY PROBLEM!!

BUT IT'S A PERISHABLE FOOD ITEM...

I WANNA KILL HER SO BAD...

BUT SHE'S NOT A TARGET, SO I CAN'T.

THIS IS THE WORST!!

Hitman Problems ────────────────── ★

Party time!

BEEP

BEEP

BEEP

THE COPS ARE GOING TO SHOW UP. WE CAN'T HAVE THAT.

UH... BUT...

THE BOSS SAID NO KILLING PEOPLE WE DON'T HAVE CONTRACTS FOR...

THAT YOU CAN KILL SOMEONE.

PROVE TO ME...

SO SHOW ME.

BEEP

BEEP

BEEP

HEY, LADY!! WHAT THE HELL ARE YOU DOING?!!

I'MMA KILL YOUR ASS!! STOP THE DAMN CAR!

WHAT THE HECK?

WE DON'T HAVE TO KILL THEM!...

BA-BLAM BLAM BLAM

SKREEE

PSHEW

OHHH WELLLL!!

BOSS'S ORDERS!

Wage ☆ Slave ☆ —————————————————— ☆

PSH

PSHEW

SAKURAI-SENPAI KEEPS TAKING ME ON JOBS.

THEY'RE ALL REALLY DANGEROUS SPOTS!

AH... SORRY!

I'M STILL HERE!!

HEY, NEWBIE!!

YOU STILL WITH US?!

N-NO...!! I STUCK RIGHT WITH YOU!!

I JUST DIDN'T WANT TO GET IN YOUR WAY, SO I TRIED TO GO UNNOTICED.

MAN, I COULDN'T SENSE YOU AT ALL.

WERE YOU HIDING SOMEWHERE?

SO YOU JUST TRY AND FADE INTO THE SCENERY!

LIKE... WHEN YOU'RE AVOIDING GOING TO A DRINKING PARTY...

Secrets to success! ⎯⎯⎯⎯⎯⎯⎯⎯⎯⎯⎯ ☆

EH?!

AH... SORRY...

YOU'RE A REAL PAIN...

BUT IT WAS SCARY WITH ALL THE GUNFIRE...

I GUESS I SHOULD HAVE DONE SOMETHING TO HELP...?

I MESSED UP AGAIN...

FWIP

FWIP

IF ONLY WE COULD HAVE TAKEN THEM IN TANDEM...

HAAAAAH...

 Senpai's so cool.

WAS SHE KILLED?

I DON'T SENSE **HER**, EITHER...

. . . . . .

THAT'S THE LAST OF THEM.

THIS WHOLE TIME?

SINCE YOU YELLED AT ME...

OH...

HOW LONG HAVE YOU BEEN BEHIND ME?

SHOULD I HAVE SAID SOMETHING?!

I THOUGHT YOU NOTICED!

I...I'M SORRY!!

Report ● Inform ● Consult ———————— ☆

She's great at blending in!

005

MY CO-WORKER SAKURAI-SAN...

REALLY DISLIKES ME.

SO I'M STUCK LOOKING AFTER THE NEWBIE...

SO, THANKS FOR TRAINING ME!!

UM... I'LL DO MY BEST...

UNLIKE THE BOSS...

HE DOESN'T HAVE ANY FAITH IN A FORMER OFFICE WORKER LIKE ME.

I'LL KILL YOU.

IF YOU GET IN MY WAY...

I'M GONNA CROAK!

Ribbited With Fear ⎯⎯⎯⎯⎯⎯⎯⎯⎯⎯ ☆

Happy Kanako's
Killer Life

Gosh darn dog-gone it!!

**Happy Kanako's
Killer Life**

This is
un-bun-
lievable
!!

You can do it!

I'll never lie again! ─────────────────────── ☆

☆ ──────────────── **Back then, I was always lying.**

Ah! ————————————————————— ☆

My parents were so proud of me back then!

Bonus

THANK YOU, SIR!!

AH, YES, SIR!!

HEY, NISHINO.

MAKE SURE YOU DON'T OVERDO IT, ALL RIGHT?

VRRRN

LOOK AT ME! THEY ALL SAID I WAS HOPELESS! NOW I'M A HITMAN!

I DEFINITELY CAN'T TELL MOM...

Mom

VRRRN

VRRRN

I've got a *baaad* feeling about this! ⎯⎯⎯⎯ ☆

Happy Kanako's
Killer Life

Whoa, that's turtley nuts!

Happy Kanako's
Killer Life

Oh no you armadill-dn't!

☆ ——————————— **You're not going home tonight!**

SOMETHING HAPPENED THIS MORNING...

OH. UH. WELL.

WHAT'S UP, NISHINO?

YOU SEEM A LITTLE SPACEY.

THE HOROSCOPE SAID I MIGHT MEET MY SPECIAL SOMEONE TODAY!

SO SURELY...

I SHOULD JUST FORGET ABOUT IT!

GOSH DARN DANG DOG-NABBIT!

HAVE AT HIM.

TODAY'S TARGET.

NOOOOOOOOOOO!

OHHHHHHHHHHHHHH

Classic shoujo manga trope, engage!

DID HE JUST RUN INTO ME ON PURPOSE?

WHOA, WHOA, WHAT THE HAWK?!

YOU THINK I'M AFRAID TO TELL YOU OFF?

YOU THINK I'LL JUST LET IT GO?

JUST BECAUSE I'M LITTLE AND FEMALE...

AND OKAY, KIND OF WEAK LOOKING...

I'M PRETTY SURE THAT'S JUST COLD-BLOODED MURDER.

GOSH, I WANNA KILL HIM!

BUT IF THERE'S NO CONTRACT...

WHY IS IT SO TOUGH TO RESIST?!

UHHHHGH!

☆——————— Adulting is hard.

004

6:58
1 Gemini

...y day!
...eign is Gemini
...ut for love!!

Today's lucky sign is Gemini, the twins!!

Be on the lookout for love!!

SOME-HOW...

LIFE FEELS *EASIER* AS A HITMAN.

I SHOULD KEEP MY EYES OPEN FOR OTHER POSSIBILITIES WHILE I CAN.

BUT BEING A HITMAN IS DANGEROUS.

AT MY OLDER, CRAPPIER JOB...

I DIDN'T EVEN HAVE TIME TO WATCH THE DAILY HOROSCOPE!

SLAM

OOOF!!

Heh.

Beast Mode Activated ─────────── ☆

☆ ——————————————— **She's still claiming it's a mi-stake!**

Slippy McSlipperson, slip slidin' away! ————————— ☆

AND THEN HE DUMPED HER.

HE KEPT FOOLING AROUND ON HER...

THE CLIENT IS A FORMER GIRLFRIEND.

HERE'S YOUR FIRST TARGET.

WORK'S BEEN A LITTLE LIGHT LATELY. WE GOTTA TAKE WHAT WE CAN GET.

I TOLD YOU: WE'LL KILL ANYONE.

EH?! THAT'S IT??

LOOKING FOR A CHANCE TO GET A GIRL DRUNK SO THAT HE CAN TAKE HER HOME.

THE KIND OF FRAT BRO WHO GETS PLASTERED EVERY NIGHT...

OKAY, SURE, HE LOOKS LIKE A BRAT.

BUT HE'S JUST SOME COLLEGE KID!

HE DESERVES TO *DIE*?

BUT DOES THAT MEAN...

☆ ———————————————— Can I really?

SO I QUIT MY AWFUL DAY JOB...

AND STARTED WORKING AS A HITMAN.

I'M NISHINO KANAKO!

THANKS FOR THIS OPPORTUNITY.

STARTING TODAY...

YOU'LL BE KILLING THE FIRST OF COUNTLESS PEOPLE.

YAKUZA, POLITICIANS, CEOs...

WHOEVER THE CLIENT WANTS.

CAN I REALLY DO THIS...?

OH, DEAR. OH, DEAR. OH, DEER!

HEARING HIM SAY IT ALOUD HAS ME WORRIED.

SCARY STUFF!

No Worries! ──────────────────── ☆

NISHINO...

YOU REALLY HAVE A KNACK FOR THIS WORK.

YOU MAY HAVE APPLIED HERE BY ACCIDENT...

BUT WE'D LOVE TO HAVE YOU.

NOT TO MENTION I CAME IN TODAY TOTALLY INTENDING TO QUIT!!

I WOULDN'T BE ABLE TO TELL MY PARENTS WHAT I DO...

I CAN'T BELIEVE MY EARS!

SO.

YOU IN?

WAIT! I SHOULD BE GOING TO THE COPS...—

BUT I'VE NEVER FELT... **WANTED...** IN A JOB BEFORE.

I'M IN!!

⭐ ——————————————— **Sorry, Mom!**

HUH?

THAT WAS YOUR FIRST TIME...

KILLING SOMEONE?

HE'S A HUNDRED TIMES SCARIER THAN OFFICE JOB ASSHAT BOSS!!

S-sorry!!

MY NEW HITMAN BOSS.

EEEEK!!

WELL.

I GUESS YOU'RE A NATURAL.

!!

☆ ————————— **Oh no he armadill-dn't!!**

002

I FELT SO LITTLE WHEN I PULLED THAT TRIGGER.

I GUESS IT BEATS JOB HUNTING.

JUST LIKE THAT, I BECAME A HITMAN.

BLAAARGH!

BUT AFTER, I JUST...

KEPT REMEM- BERING.

Boy, you can really toss 'em back!

I KEEP REMEM- BERING--

AFTER KILLING SOMEONE!!

HOW GREAT EVERY DRINK TASTED...

Watch out for hangovers. ──────── ☆

☆ ——————————— **Let's get sloshed!**

WHA-AAT ?!

ALL RIGHT. TIME FOR YOUR FIRST TEST.

USE THIS TO TAKE OUT THE TARGET.

THEY'LL MAKE IT LOOK LIKE AN ACCIDENT.

WE'VE GOT A CLEAN-UP CREW READY.

YOUR TARGET IS YOUR FORMER BOSS.

WE LOOKED INTO YOUR WORK HIS-TORY.

HE'D ALWAYS RUB MY NECK, AND HE YELLED SO MUCH. HE'D BERATE ME IN FRONT OF THE OTHERS IF ANYTHING WENT WRONG, THEN LEER AT--

MY LAST BOSS, THOUGH, JEEZ.

I CAN'T JUST KILL SOMEONE!!

NO WAY!! NO CHANCE IN SHELL!

BLAM

MY FINGER SLIPPED! ☆

AHHHH!! YIKES!

Full Marks! ──────────── ☆

WAIT.

UH...

Though you look pretty unassuming.

THAT SAID, YOU DID MANAGE TO TRACK US DOWN.

SO CLEARLY YOU'VE GOT SOME SKILLS.

MAYBE IF I APOLOGIZE, THEY'LL LET ME COME BACK...

I WAS SO MAD AT MY OLD BOSS I JUST HIT THE PHONE BOOK STARTING WITH "A."

THIS IS AN ASSASSIN FIRM?

GET OTTER HERE!

BUT HEY, IT'S A COMPETITIVE MARKET.

Times are changing.

WE DIDN'T USED TO OFFER BENEFITS...

HOURS ARE TEN TO SEVEN, PLUS YOU GET WEEKENDS OFF.

OUR STARTING SALARY IS SIX HUNDRED THOUSAND YEN.

BA-D-U-M-P

WHA...?

★ ————————————————— **Unexpected Benefits!**

001

MY LAST JOB WAS THE WORST.

SO I QUIT.

Don't be a baby! Quitting already? Typical millennial.

THAT SUCKED.

IN MY LAST POSITION AT THE ADVERTISING AGENCY, I--

I'M NISHINO KANAKO.

BUT MY PARENTS WILL BE WORRYING SOON...

SO, IT'S BACK TO JOB HUNTING.

ANYHOW, YOU EVER KILLED ANYONE?

HEY. UH.

YOU...DO REALIZE WE'RE HITMEN, RIGHT?

SAY WHAT?

No Experience Needed! ⎯⎯⎯⎯⎯⎯⎯⎯⎯⎯⎯⎯⎯⎯ ☆

Happy Kanako's
Killer Life

you gotter be kidding me!!

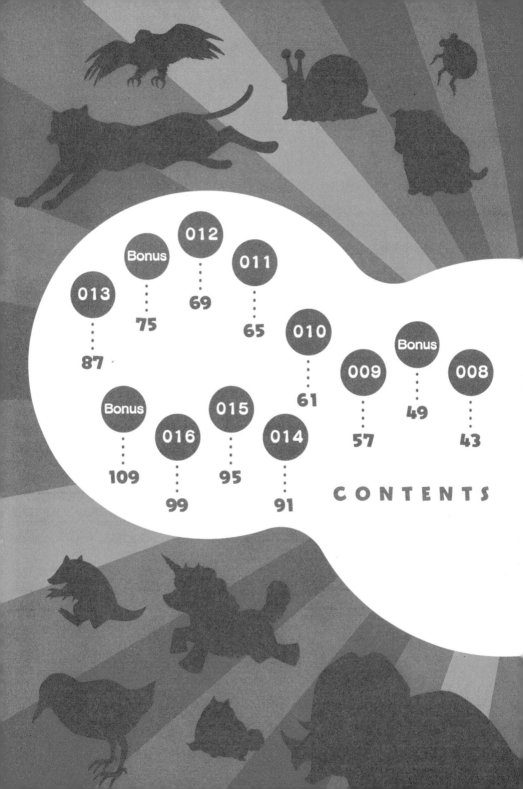

CONTENTS

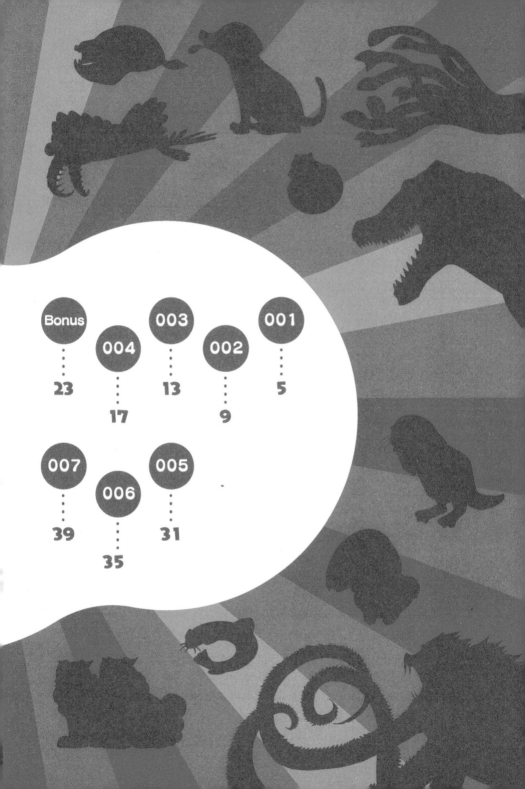

story & art by:
TOSHIYA WAKABAYASHI